My Activity Book About NATURE

(Originally published as *Exploring Nature*)

By John Mongillo

GROSSET & DUNLAP
A FILMWAYS COMPANY
Publishers • New York

1977 Printing
ISBN: 0-448-14451-4
Copyright © 1972 by Xerox Corporation.
Printed in U.S.A. All rights reserved. This book may not
be reproduced in whole or in part in any form or format
without permission in writing from the publisher.
Grosset & Dunlap trade edition published by arrangement with
Xerox Education Publications.
XEROX® is a trademark of Xerox Corporation.
(Originally published under the title *EXPLORING NATURE*)

CONTENTS

5	Foreword	28	Capture Houseflies
7	Stump Yourself	29	Poking in a Dirt Pile
8	Reading the Age of Trees	30	Make a Bucket-Microscope
9	Bring the Outside In!	31	Insect Homes
10	Iron a Leafy Mat	32	Make a Cage for Insects
12	Observing Salamanders	33	Draw a Praying Mantis
13	Go for Galls	34	Collect Caterpillars
14	"C" Is for Cone	35	Be a Cloud-Watcher
16	Be a Turtle Watcher	36	Make a Rain Gauge
17	Growing Twigs	37	Mud Splash Cards
18	Collect Old Christmas Trees	38	Make a Weather Vane
19	Does a Toad Change Color?	40	How Fast Does the Wind Blow?
20	Explore the Edge of a Pond	41	Fun at the Beach
22	Set Up a Pond Aquarium	42	Try to Find a Whelk
23	Watch a Frog	43	A Picture Guide to Shells
24	Simple Bird Feeders	44	Peek Through a Waterscope
25	Build a Birdhouse	45	Hunt for Animal Tracks
26	Become a Rock Hound	46	I See Icicles
27	Make an Ant Village	47	Frosty Fun

foreword

Exploring the outdoors is fun. And if you look, listen, smell, and touch, you can discover many exciting things.

This book suggests lots of things to do outdoors. For example, you can look at a woolly caterpillar with a homemade bucket-microscope, capture flies for your pet salamander, peek under the water with a waterscope — or even iron a leafy mat!

When exploring the outdoors, protect and care for the animals, insects, and plants that share the world you live in. And do something nice — take along a grown-up!

STUMP YOURSELF

In the woods you can hear birds, touch ferns and moss, smell trees, and see all kinds of plants and animals.

Why not take a camera to shoot pictures of what you see? If you have a tape recorder, take it to record what you hear. Field glasses, a magnifying lens, a pencil, and a notebook are also useful tools. Keep alert and, remember, never go far into the woods by yourself.

While you're in the woods, look for a fallen log or dead tree stump. Study it carefully. Can you find any insects living in the wood?

You may see signs of fungus growing on the bark. Fungus gets food from the wood. Sketch the different kinds of fungi.

Dig around the log or stump. You may find grubs, beetles, earthworms and ants. Keep your eyes open for a salamander or a newt. These small animals like damp places where they can feed on the insects.

Write about the different kinds of living things you see in and around dead wood.

U.S. Forest Service photo

Fallen trees in 105-year-old stand of lodgepole pine.

U.S. Forest Service photo

Velvet top fungus on western white pine.

Study the dead wood carefully.

Look for a fallen log or dead tree stump.

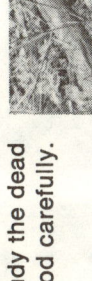

Reading the Age of Trees

Do you know how to discover the age of a tree? All you need is a tree stump that has been cut across.

Look at the light and dark rings on the stump. The light rings show the growth of the tree during the spring. The dark rings show the growth of the tree during the summer. Each light and dark ring shows one year's growth.

To find out how old the tree was when it was cut, count the dark rings, which are easier to see. Count the rings from the center of the stump to the outside. How old is the tree?

A tree stump can tell you the age of the tree. Look at the light and dark rings on the stump.

Each light and dark ring shows one year's growth.

bring the outside in!

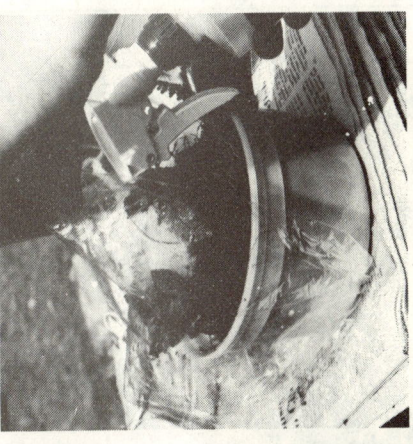

You can make a terrarium in a wide-mouth jar. Set plants in the soil, water lightly, and cover with plastic.

To bring a little of the woods into your home, make a woodland terrarium.

Use an aquarium tank, a wide-mouth jar, or a refrigerator bowl for a container. Put a layer of coarse gravel on the bottom. Add some garden soil; don't pack it too tightly. Bury some small pieces of charcoal in the soil. The charcoal will help to prevent the soil from turning sour.

Now set some woodland plants such as moss and ferns into the soil. These plants may be as near as a neighboring woodlot. Sprinkle the plants with water. Not too much! Cover the top of your terrarium with plastic wrap. Set it in a spot that is out of direct sunlight and away from the heat.

If your terrarium is large and you decide to keep a toad or a salamander, use a screen on top instead of the plastic wrap. Add a small dish of water if animals are to live in it.

Remember, don't overcrowd your terrarium with too many plants or animals. Too much water will kill the plants. Watch what goes on in the terrarium each week. Keep a record of what you see.

A large terrarium can be a home to a toad or salamander.

9

iron a leafy mat

AEP photo

With the help of nature you can make breakfast table mats in the autumn. Take some friends outdoors to gather leaves. When you get home, sort the leaves and pick out the most colorful ones.

Place the leaves on a sheet of wax paper. Lay another sheet of wax paper over the leaves. Ask mother to set the iron on "warm."

Spread a sheet of newspaper over the wax paper. Use the warm iron to press over the newspaper very carefully. Press down as you move the iron back and forth. Do this four or five times. The heat of the iron will melt the wax on the paper.

Lift the newspaper to make sure the corners of the wax paper are ironed together. Now hold your leafy mat up to the light. The two pieces of wax paper have sealed your leaves inside.

Use your mat on the breakfast table. The mat will look great taped to a window in the sunlight also.

Sort out the most colorful leaves for your table mat.

Press leaves between pieces of wax paper.

11

observing salamanders

Salamanders make fine pets. They live in places that are damp and moist. Look for one under rocks, leaves, fallen logs, or tree roots. The best time to collect a salamander is the spring or summer. In the winter they burrow into the ground.

One salamander is all you need for a large terrarium. Each day fill the water dish in your terrarium with fresh water. Keep the terrarium in a cool place. Keep a screen on top of the terrarium to let air in and to keep your salamander from getting out. Feed the animal live insects and worms. Remove any uneaten food.

Watch your salamander and record what it does each day. After studying the salamander, return the animal to its natural home — the woods.

UPI photo

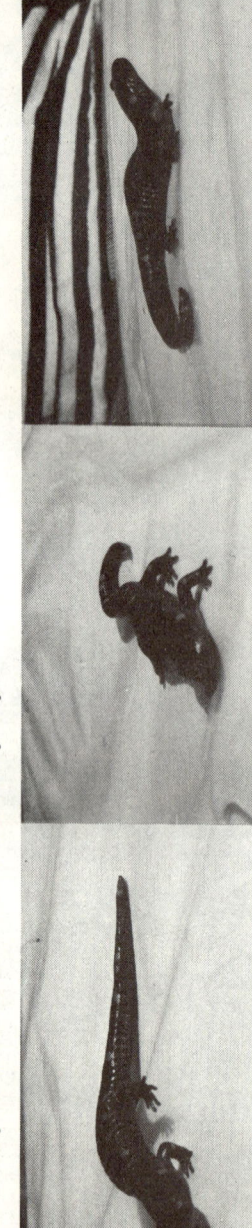
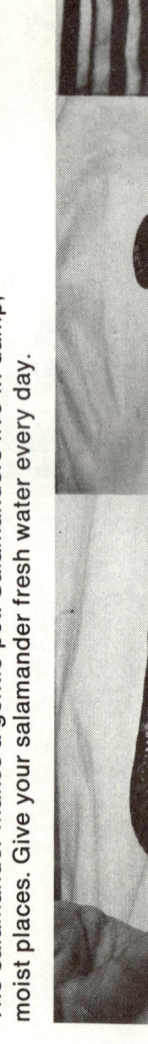

Spotted salamander is shown larger than life-size.

The salamander makes a gentle pet. Salamanders live in damp, moist places. Give your salamander fresh water every day.

Go for galls

When studying trees and plants, you may see some strange things growing on stems and leaves. These may be galls. Galls come in all shapes, colors and sizes. Some are ball-shaped, some are woolly, some are lumpy.

How does the gall form? It can happen when an insect lays its eggs inside a part of a plant. As the eggs grow this part of the plant swells up, forming a gall. The gall serves as food for the growing insects. When the insects are big enough, they chew a hole through the gall and fly away. Wasps and flies are among the insects that cause galls.

Look for galls on willows, oak trees, hickory trees and on goldenrod plants. If you find one you can reach, try this experiment. Cover the gall with a nylon stocking. Use a rubber band or string to keep it tight. The stocking will hold the insects when they come out of the gall.

After studying the insects, let them fly away.

Look for galls on growing plants, especially oaks. The insects have chewed their way out of this gall. Flies and wasps are among the insects that cause galls.

U.S. Forest Service photo

"c" is for cone

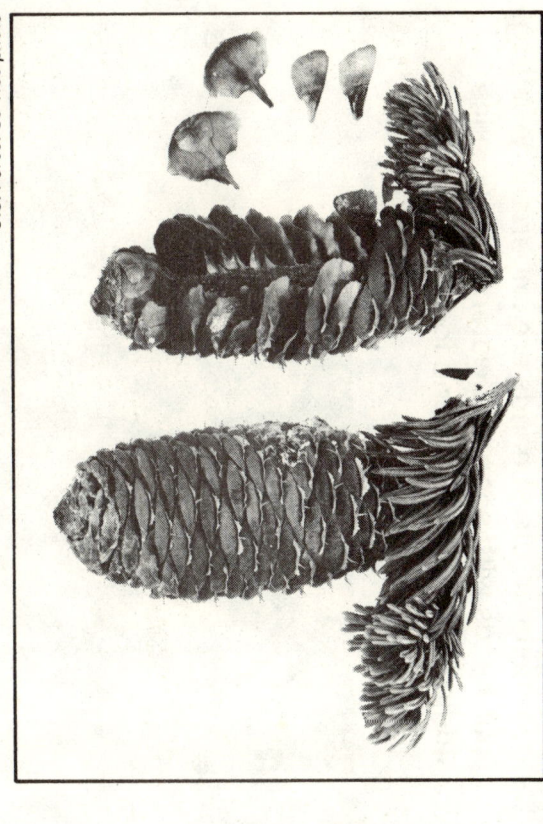

U.S. Forest Service photo

Pull the scales of a cone to look for seeds.

While hiking in the woods, collect some cones. Cones come from different kinds of evergreen trees such as fir, pine, and spruce. The cones in the photo are from a balsam fir tree.

Look carefully at the scales on the cone. Pull apart some of the scales of a cone. You may see seeds or places where seeds once were beneath the scales.

If you find a seed, try growing it in your terrarium or in your garden. Keep a record of how long it takes the seed to sprout and begin to grow.

Cones on a balsam fir tree.

15

be a turtle watcher

Most water turtles swallow their food only while they are underwater. So if you plan to feed and care for a turtle, find out what kind of turtle you have.

Observe how the turtle moves. What kinds of food does it like best? After caring for your turtle, let it go in the same place where you found it. Remember, clean hands are important. Washing your hands with soap and water make science studies safer for you — and for the turtle.

Wash your hands after you handle a turtle.

Peter Mongillo photo

The spotted turtle shown here lives near ponds or streams.

Turtles are interesting creatures to study. Some live near the water. Some live in the desert. Others live in the woods. For example, you'll find the spotted turtle near ponds, in swamps, or streams. Some turtles can be kept in a large box. Cover the bottom of the box with soil, gravel and moss. Set a shallow water dish into the soil. Turtles have to be fed only a few times a week. They eat earthworms, insects, and sometimes lettuce, apples, and bananas.

16

Growing Twigs

During the late winter and early spring, study twigs on different trees and shrubs. Have the buds begun to swell?

Ask a grown-up to help you cut a few twigs to bring indoors. Cut each twig off at an angle; do not cut it straight across. Bring the twigs home and place each one in a jar of water.

In a few days or weeks, the leaf buds of the twigs may open. Later, the twigs may even begin to grow roots. If roots do appear, keep the twig until late spring and then plant it in your garden. Keep track of how the twig grows during the summer.

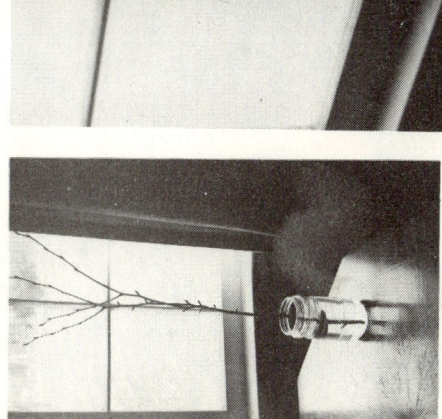
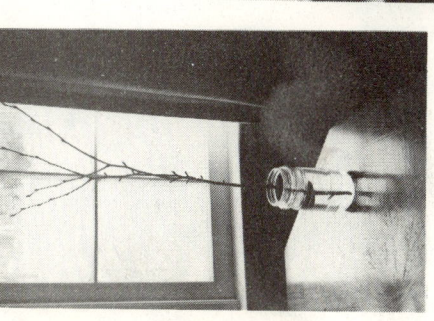
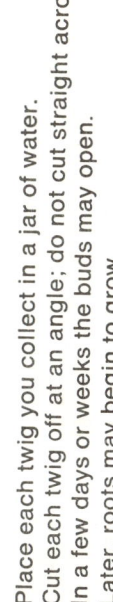

Place each twig you collect in a jar of water.
Cut each twig off at an angle; do not cut straight across.
In a few days or weeks the buds may open.
Later, roots may begin to grow.

collect old CHRISTMAS TREES

What do you do with old Christmas trees? You share them with needy forest friends! The trees can be used as brush shelters for different kinds of wildlife.

After the holidays, some people take their trees to a wildlife area. There the trees are stacked in piles. Usually the trees are stacked up against a pole. In time the brush pile will become a home for small animals and birds.

If you would like to work on a project like this, check with the neighborhood adults. It's a good way to share your Christmas tree!

What do you do with old Christmas trees?
Piled together, the trees make a shelter for wildlife.
Neighbors can share the Christmas tree project.
Small birds and animals live in the wildlife area.

does a toad change color?

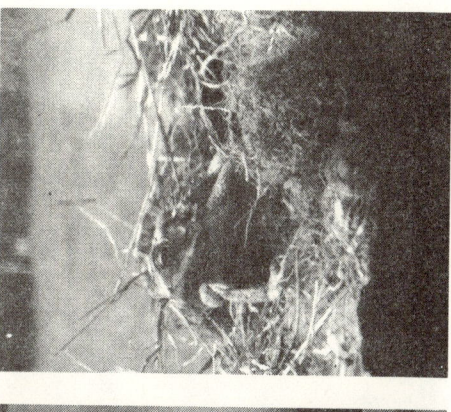

John and Peter Mongillo

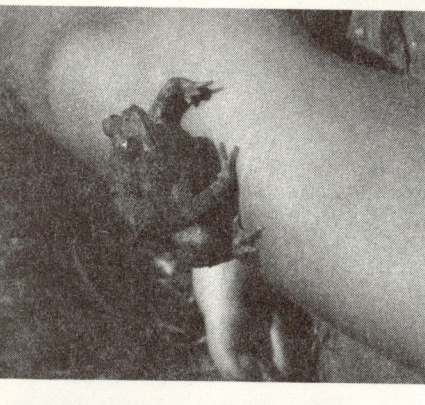

Toads come out at night to feed.

If you find a toad, keep it in a shady place.

Sometimes a toad will change color.

A dark box may help you to see the toad change color.

Toads are plentiful in many parts of the United States. Usually they come out at night to feed on insects and they are very helpful in your garden.

If you find a toad, keep it in a cool, shaded terrarium. Place a small dish of water in the terrarium. Feed the toad live earthworms, crickets, flies, or mealworms. Watch how the toad eats. Record how many insects the toad eats at one time. Feed your toad at least three times a week. Sometimes a toad will change color. To watch the color change, get a box that is all black inside. Put a screen on top. Place the toad in the box for at least one hour. Now look at the toad. Is it darker or lighter than when you put it in the box?

Next use a box that is light-colored inside. Place the toad in the box and wait an hour or so. Did the toad change color?

After studying the toad, let it go again in a shady part of the garden. Write a report on the toad or give a talk to your classmates.

19

Peabody Museum, Yale University

explore the edge of a pond

Peabody Museum, Yale University

Walking the edge of a nearby pond on a warm spring day is a good way to learn what lives in and around this watery world. Go with a grown-up and take along a pail and a net. Wear old clothes.

Find a place at the edge where you can stand safely. Look carefully and you'll see many kinds of plants and animals. Some of the animals feed on plants. And other animals feed on the plant-eaters. In the water you may see tadpoles, water striders, frogs and small fish. Now look just above the surface of the water. You may see a dragonfly catch an insect in mid-flight!

Which pond creatures did you see the most? Draw a picture of the pond and include the plants and animals. Write a story about what you saw at the pond.

Find a place where you can stand safely.

Go to the pond with a grown-up, and take a pail and a net.

21

SET UP A POND AQUARIUM

At the pond collect a few plants and animals for a pond aquarium. Make sure you have permission to do so. Use plastic containers or pails for collecting. Fill the containers with pond water. Collect a few tadpoles and some pond insects. Gather some algae-covered rocks, some pond soil and a few plants. Don't collect too much.

At home, line the bottom of a fish tank with pond soil. Set in the rocks and plants. Fill the tank with pond water. Add the tadpoles and the insects. Don't overcrowd the tank with plants and animals.

Place the tank in an area where the plants can get some sunlight. Make sure the pond water stays cool. Warm water may kill the tadpoles. As the water evaporates, add more pond water.

The tadpoles will feed on the algae that grows on plant stems and rocks. Watch the tadpoles as they grow. If you are patient, you may see them turn into tiny frogs or toads!

After caring for the creatures in your pond aquarium, return the plants and animals to their home in the pond.

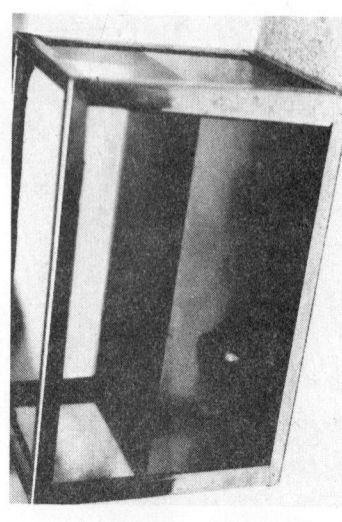

Don't overcrowd your aquarium with plants.

Peter Mongillo

In the springtime, try to capture a tadpole.

Peter Mongillo

Collect some pond soil and some plants.

AEP photo by Nils Lommerin

WATCH A FROG

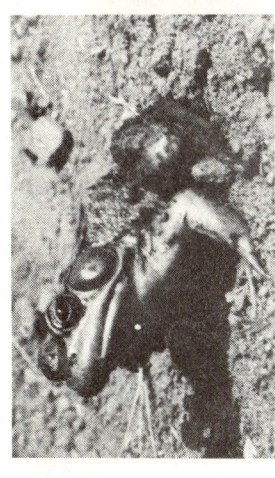

This is a bullfrog.

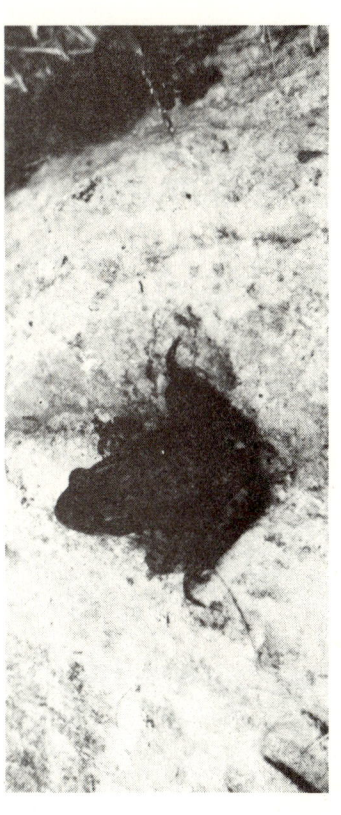
Handle your frog gently.

Frogs are good swimmers.

Frogs need a place to get up out of the water.

Find a frog. Make a study of it. But before you collect a frog, ask permission to be sure that you can.

A frog can be kept in an aquarium tank. Fill the tank with about four inches of pond water. Don't use water from the faucet!

Place some pebbles or rocks at one end of the tank. Pile the pebbles high enough so the frog can come out of the water. Now place the frog in the tank. Handle it gently. Keep a screen on top of the tank.

Feed the frog live insects such as worms, moths, and flies. Capture the flies with a fly trap. The frog may not eat dead insects. If your frog won't eat, return him to the pond right away.

See how the frog catches food with his tongue. What insects does the frog like to eat? How does the frog swim? After watching the frog, take it back to the pond.

23

simple bird feeders

John and Peter Mongillo

Discover the many kinds of birds in your backyard. Make a simple bird feeder. Bird feeders will attract all kinds of birds during the year.

Simple bird feeders can be made out of milk cartons or plastic egg cartons. Study the photos on these pages for ideas on how to make bird feeders. Make several kinds.

Fill some of the bird feeders with wild birdseed. Fill other feeders with bread or fat trimmings. Hang the bird feeders in different parts of the backyard.

Watch the birds at your feeders for about a half hour each day. Use binoculars to watch the birds closely. Tape record their songs and chirps. Use a bird-watchers' guidebook to find out the names of the birds.

What kinds of birds eat the seeds? What birds eat the bread crumbs and fat trimmings? If possible, leave the feeders up all year long. Keep a record of the different kinds of birds that visit your feeders. How many different kinds of birds come to *your* backyard?

Wild bird seed mixtures attract many birds.

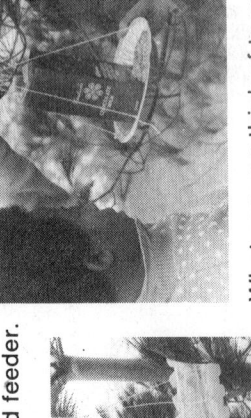

What can you think of to use as a bird feeder?

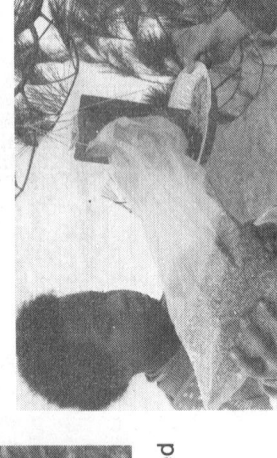

Put more seeds in the feeder when the birds have emptied it.

An empty milk carton makes a good bird feeder.

Egg cartons may be filled with bread crumbs or suet.

build a birdhouse

Here is an easy way to build a birdhouse for your backyard. All you need is an empty plastic bottle.

Wash out the bottle to make sure it is clean inside. Paint or color the outside of the birdhouse with dark colors. Cut a hole a few inches from the bottom. Add a round piece of wood below the hole for the bird to use as a perch.

Make two or three birdhouses in the late winter or early spring and put them in quiet places in the woods. Don't put them too close together, for bird families like plenty of room.

In the spring a pair of birds may use your birdhouse for raising their young. If they do, find out what kind of birds are nesting in your birdhouse.

Try using other plastic containers to make birdhouses. Use your imagination and *you* may come up with a better birdhouse!

Hang your birdhouse in a quiet place.

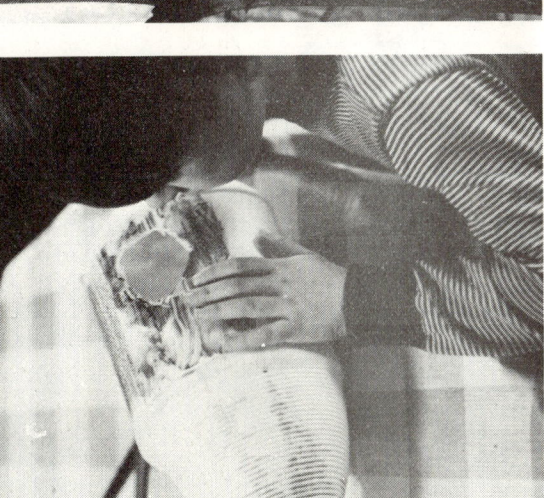

Cut a hole in the side of the bottle.

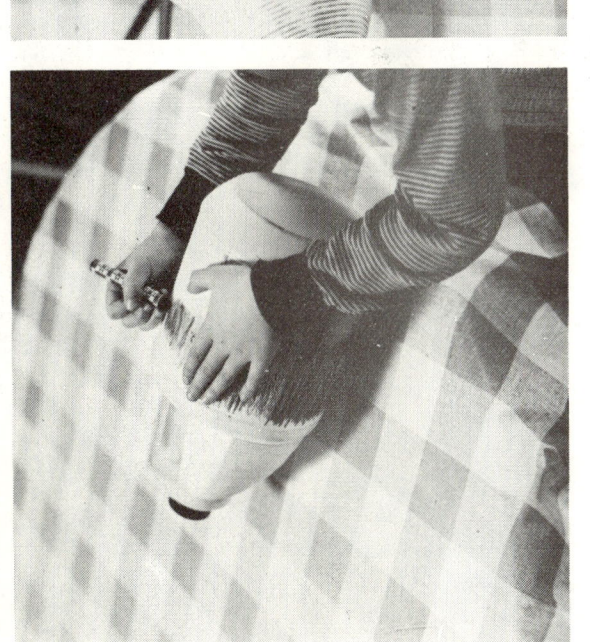

An empty plastic bottle makes a good birdhouse.

become a rock hound

A rock hound looks for unusual rocks. So whether you live in the city or the country, there are places to hunt rocks nearby.

Backyards, parks, roadsides and school grounds are good rock-hunting places. The best place is where people are building new roads or buildings. Where the ground is turned over, there are many interesting rocks. But you need permission to go into these places and you should go with a grown-up.

On your rock-hunting trip, take along a box or sack, newspaper, and a felt-tipped pen. Look for unusual rocks. When you find one, wrap it in newspaper. Write on the newspaper the name of the place where you found the rock.

At home, arrange your rocks into groups according to colors. Look at the rocks carefully with a magnifying glass. You may want to keep your rock collection in an egg carton. Later, you may want to trade some of your rocks with other rock hounds.

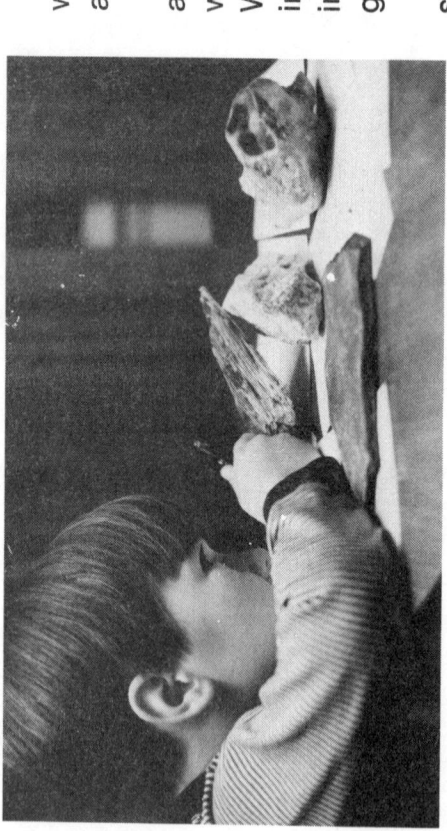

Arrange your rocks into groups according to color.

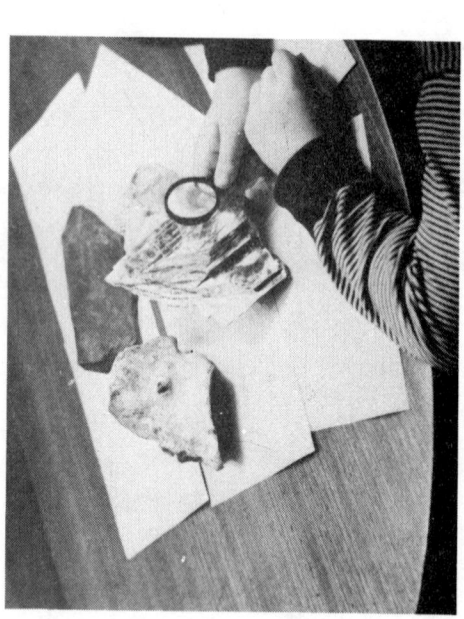

Look at the rocks carefully with a magnifying glass.

Make an Ant Village

To learn something about ants and their habits, make an ant village. Get a large glass jar and fill it with dirt to within a few inches of the top. Punch tiny holes in the jar top to let in air. Wrap some black paper around the sides of the jar. Hold the paper in place with rubber bands.

Now look for ant nests under logs or rocks. Collect a few ants and place them in the jar. Put the lid on and place the jar in a dark place. Most ants do not like light.

Every few days remove the paper to see if the ants have started to build chambers and tunnels. Keep a small piece of wet sponge in the jar for water. For food, mix some honey and water in a bottle cap and put it in the jar. For other foods, try sugar water or cracker crumbs. Watch how the ants approach their food. What kinds of food do they like best?

Make another ant village, using a plastic box filled with soil. Add some ants and a piece of wet sponge. Punch holes in a sheet of cardboard cut to fit on top of the box. Put the box in a pan of water. The water will keep the ants from escaping.

Place a bottle cap filled with sugar water and some dead insects on top of the cardboard. Watch the ants as they come through the holes and move about on the cardboard. Write a report on what the ants do.

American Economic Foundation

This is a carpenter ant.

Ray Broekel for Weekly Reader

You can make an ant village in a jar or in a plastic box.

Capture Houseflies

How many flies do you think you can catch in the great outdoors? To make a good flytrap, get a small jar, a funnel, and a ripe banana. Put a piece of banana into the jar. Cover the jar with the funnel.

Take your flytrap outdoors. The flies will come right down into the jar to eat the banana. After you capture the flies, cover the funnel with paper. Poke some pinholes in the paper to let the flies breathe.

If you are lucky enough to see the flies lay eggs, watch the changes the fly goes through as it grows from egg to adult. Keep a record of what you see. Each day watch what happens in the jar.

Observe the body parts of the insect. Draw what you see. How does the fly behave when you shine a light into the jar?

Catching live flies is a good way to get food for your pet toad, frog, salamander, or praying mantis. Always wash your hands after handling flies or other insects.

USDA, Agricultural Research Magazine

These house flies are shown larger than life-size.

A glass jar, a funnel, and a banana make a good fly trap.

poking in a dirt pile

Collecting insects can be done in the summer, fall, spring, and even in the winter months. Insects can be found on leaves, in grass piles, and in the garden soil. Even tearing off a bit of tree bark may yield small insects.

Ask permission to dig up a few inches of soil. Bring the soil indoors and put it on a sheet of white paper. Now slowly pick away at the soil. Carefully examine it with a magnifying lens.

As you're poking away, you may find a small "zoo" of insects such as spiders, centipedes, ants, beetles, grubs, and other insects. Count and keep records of the kinds of insects you see.

Wells Elementary School

Many kinds of insects may live in the dirt.

Dig up a few inches of soil and bring it indoors.

29

Make a bucket-microscope

Would you like to see an insect up close? To make a bucket-microscope, get an old plastic bucket. You might even use the kind that carry-out fried chicken comes in!

Cut three holes in the sides of the bucket, big enough to get your hands through. Now get a large sheet of plastic wrap. Place it on top of the bucket, making sure the plastic hangs over the sides. Place an elastic band snugly around the plastic wrap. Make sure it's tight. Pour water slowly onto the plastic. The plastic will start to stretch. It will sag down into the bucket.

Place an insect on the bottom of the bucket. Look through the water. What do you see? Add more water to the plastic. Does the insect get larger?

The water acts as a magnifying lens!

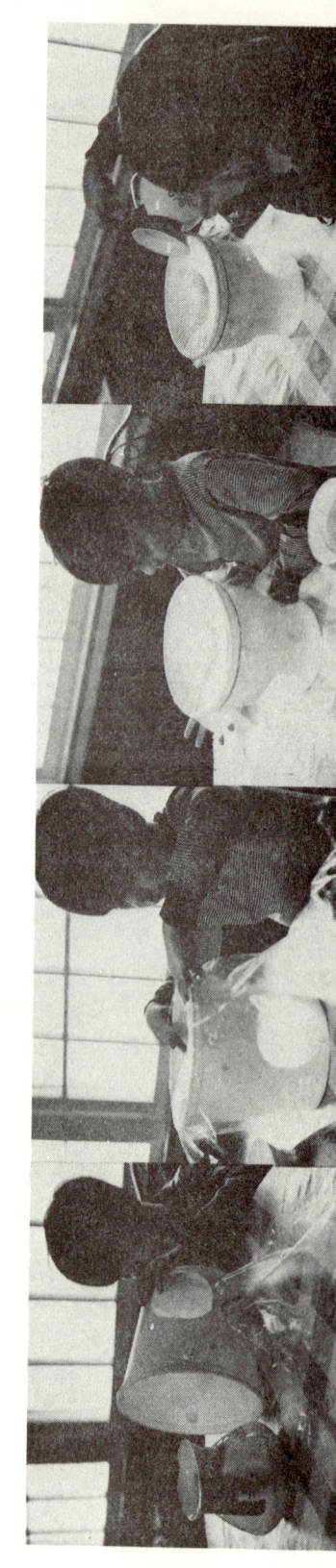

Cut holes in the sides of a plastic bucket. Put a sheet of plastic wrap over the top. Fasten the plastic wrap with a large elastic band. Pour some water onto the plastic and look through it.

Insect Homes

To make "homes" for small insects, just place a piece of wood, a stone, or bricks on the ground in different places.

Wait a week or two, then lift up the "house." Do you see any insects? If so, can you name them? What do the insects do when you pick up their house? What kinds of food do you think they like? In which of the homes did you find the most insects?

A piece of wood, a stone, and bricks make insect "homes."

What insects live under the bricks?

What insects live under the wood?

What insects live under the stone?

make a cage for insects

Going insect hunting? To make an insect cage, all you need are some wire screening, pins, and a box or bowl.

Roll the piece of screening into the shape of a cone. Pin the sides together with safety pins. For the bottom of the cage use a box or bowl. To give your insect water, wet some paper toweling and place it on the bottom of the cage.

The cage is a good place to watch a praying mantis, a cricket, or a grasshopper. Observe your insect with a magnifying glass, then let it go.

Give your insect water, watch him, and then let him go.

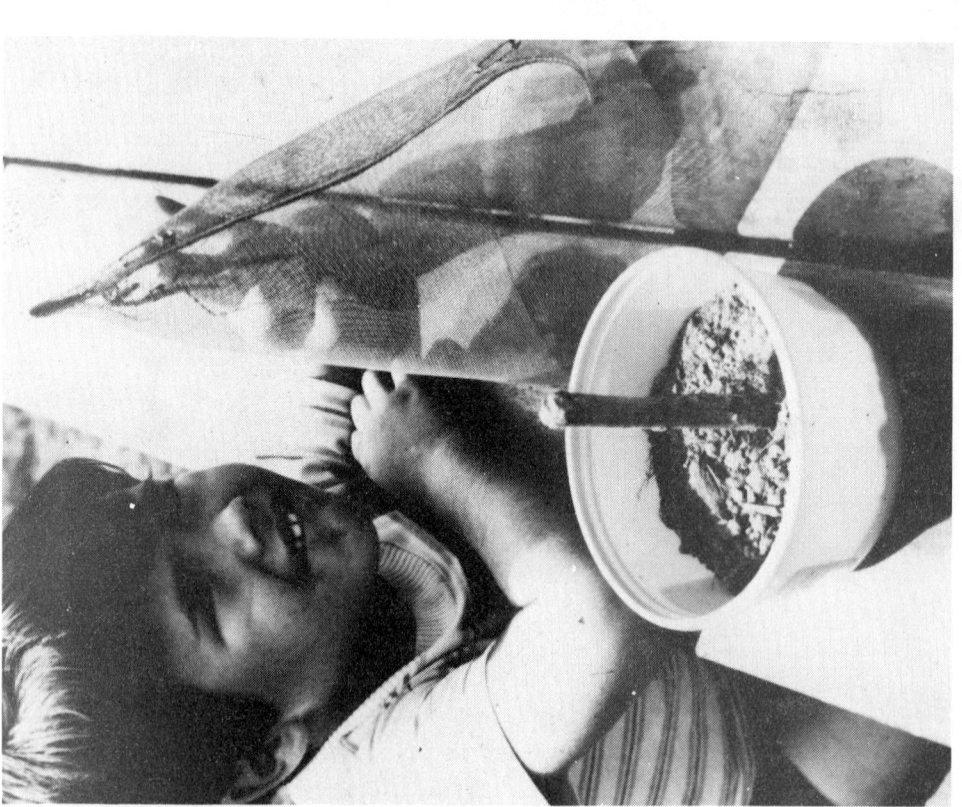

To make an insect cage, use screening, pins, and a bowl.

DRAW A PRAYING MANTIS

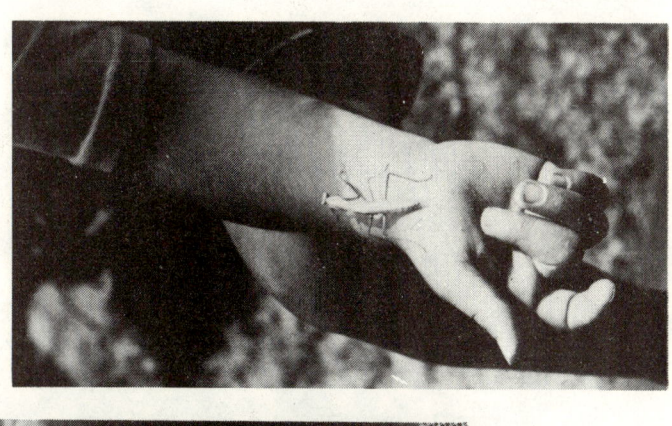

After studying it, set the mantis free in the garden.

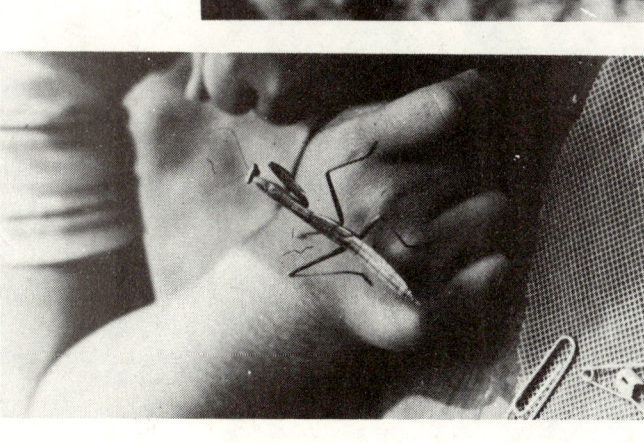

The praying mantis is one of nature's strangest creatures.

The praying mantis is surely one of nature's strangest looking creatures. It is the only known insect which can turn its head to look backwards. Some mantises are green, some are gray, some brown. They may grow as large as four to six inches long.

The praying mantis is a good insect to have in your garden. It has a big appetite and it destroys many harmful insects. The praying mantis eats houseflies, grasshoppers, caterpillars, crickets, and moths. The mantises are harmless to people.

If you find a praying mantis, put it in a jar or a screen cage so you can watch it for a few days. Set a capful of water in the cage and get a good supply of insects to feed the praying mantis. What insects does the mantis prefer to eat? Will it eat from your hand?

Use a magnifying glass and look at the large forelegs of the praying mantis. Draw a picture of this strange-looking creature. After a day or two, set the mantis free where it can do the most good — in the flower garden.

33

collect caterpillars

In the springtime when the leaves are fresh and green, you'll see caterpillars crawling up trees, on bushes, and in the grass. They have hatched from egg masses and they are looking for something to eat.

Hunt for caterpillars feeding on leafy twigs. Cut off the twigs, making sure the caterpillar stays on them. At home, get a large box, a quart glass jar, and some cotton. Fill the jar with water and stick the twigs into the jar. The water will keep the twigs fresh. Now place the cotton around the opening of the jar to keep the caterpillar from falling into the water.

Put the jar in a box filled with dirt. Keep the box in a place where the twigs will get sunlight. Record what the caterpillar does each day.

In time, the caterpillar may begin to spin a cocoon. If so, sprinkle the cocoon lightly with water. This will keep it from drying up. With a little luck, you may see a moth come out of the cocoon.

U.S. Dept. of Agriculture

These caterpillars will spin cocoons and then emerge as moths.

be a cloud-watcher

Which way are the clouds moving today? Are they going north or east? Weathermen have to know cloud direction to predict the weather. They do this by using a cloud direction instrument called a nephoscope. You can make one by following these directions.

Get a sheet of cardboard about ten inches square, some crayons, and a square mirror. Draw lines and letters on the cardboard as shown in the photos. The letters stand for north, east, south and west. Put the mirror in the center of the cardboard.

Take the cloud instrument outdoors and put it on a flat surface. Turn it until the side marked "N" faces north. Ask a grown-up with a compass to help you find which direction is north.

Now look into the mirror as a cloud passes over. In which direction is the cloud moving? If the image of the cloud moves across the mirror at the north position, the cloud is being blown to the north. Therefore, the wind is coming from *the* south.

Keep a daily record of the cloud direction. At the same time, keep track of the weather. In which direction did the clouds move on sunny days? In which direction were the clouds moving on stormy days?

Make a cloud instrument from a piece of square cardboard.

Mark the four sides with the letters N, S, E, and W. Place a mirror in the center of your cloud instrument. Place it outdoors on a flat surface, and watch the clouds.

35

MAKE A RAIN GAUGE

You can measure the amount of rain that falls if you have a rain gauge. A can, a tall jar, a strip of paper, and some glue are all that you need to make a simple rain gauge. This rain gauge will give you some idea of the amount of rain that falls during a storm.

1. Pour one inch of water into the can. Make sure the can has a flat bottom. Use a ruler to measure the water.

2. Pour the water from the can into a tall, narrow glass jar. Paste a strip of paper down the side of the jar. Make a line on the paper where the water level is. This mark will show one inch of rain water.

3. Divide the space between this water level mark and the bottom of the jar into eight parts. Each mark will show one-eighth inch of rainfall.

4. Place the can outdoors about two feet off the ground. After each rainfall, pour the water out of the can into the glass jar. How many inches of rain did you get? Keep a chart of the amount of rainfall you get in one month.

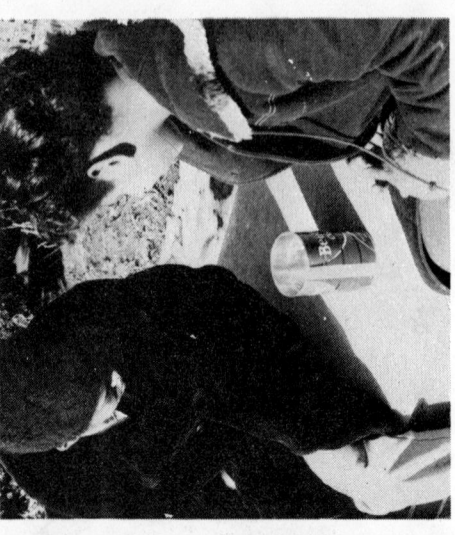

Peter Mongillo

After a storm, pour the rain water from the can into the jar.

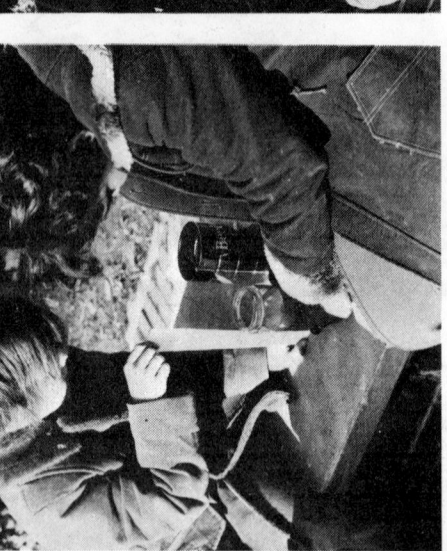

Mark the water level on a strip of paper pasted to the jar.

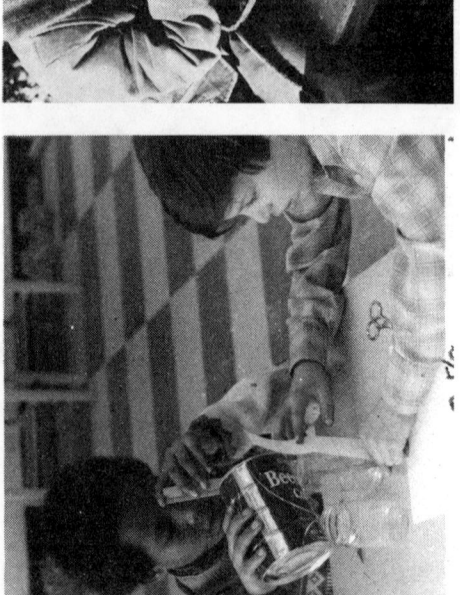

Pour the measured inch of water from the can into a jar.

mud splash cards

When it rains, the force of the raindrops breaks up the soil and splashes it away. How much splash erosion takes place in your backyard when it rains?

To find out, make some splash cards from pieces of cardboard, thumbtacks, and short sticks. Tack a sheet of cardboard to each stick. Push the sticks into the ground in different places, such as in the grass, in sand, and on a hillside.

After a rainfall, examine each card. Where does most splash erosion take place? In the grassy area? In the sandy area? On the hillside?

Make new cards and set them out in the same places. Check them again after a storm. Does splash erosion take place after each rainfall? What can you do to help prevent splash erosion?

Tack a piece of cardboard to a stick to make a splash card.

Set the splash cards outside in different places.

During a rainfall, does mud splash from the grassy area?

Make a new set of cards, and set them out again.

37

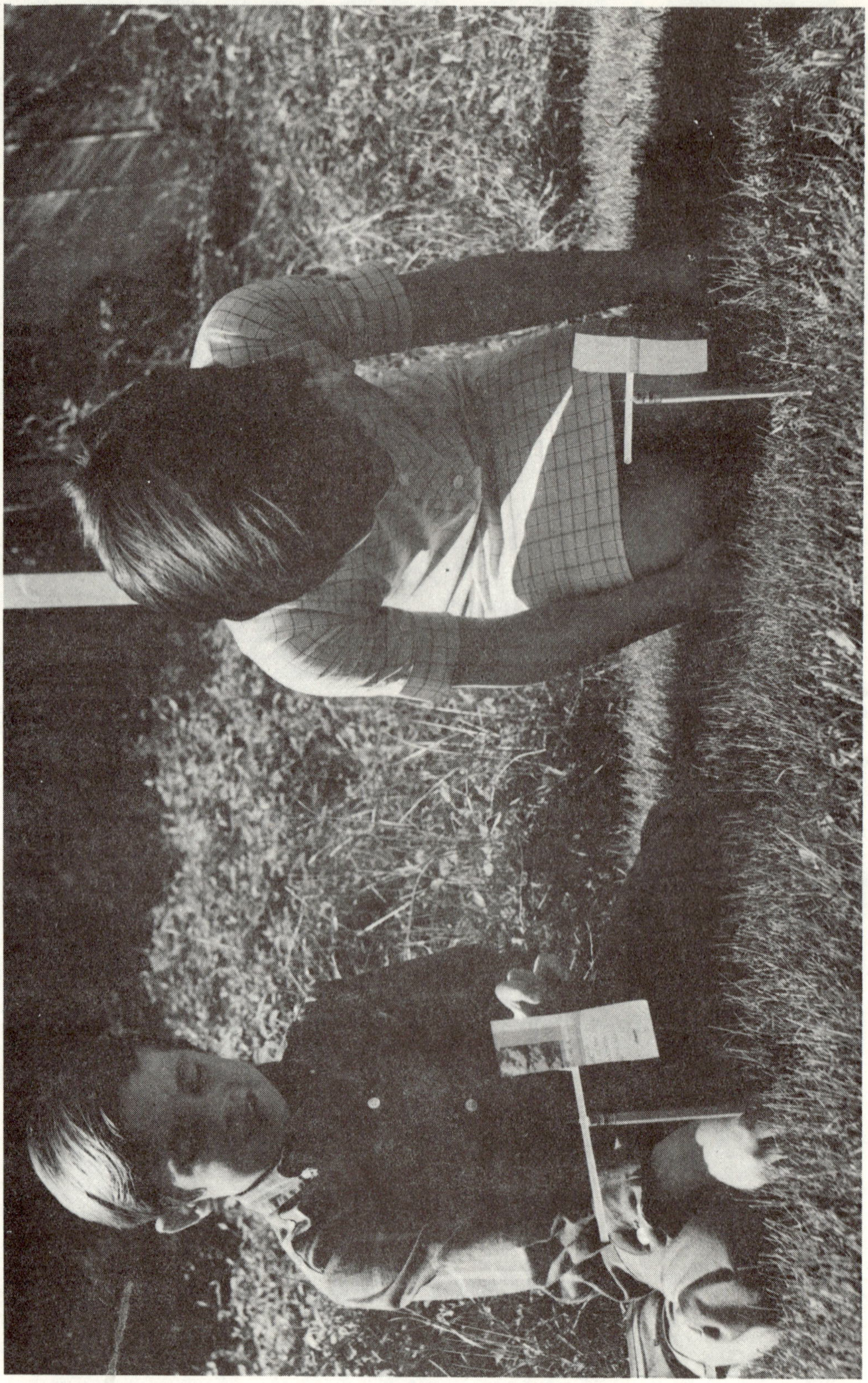

MAKE A WEATHER VANE

Nils Lommerin for AEP

Weather watchers use weather vanes to study the wind. The weathervane points into the direction of the wind.

To make a simple weather vane, you'll need a pencil with an eraser, a strip of paper, a soda straw, a straight pin, and glue.

Glue the paper strip to the side of the straw as shown in the photo. Push the pin through the straw into the eraser tip. Leave enough space for the straw to swing around in the wind.

Make several weather vanes and take them outdoors. Put them in different places in the backyard. Keep a record of wind direction and the kind of weather.

Which way does the wind blow on a sunny day? Which way does the wind blow when storm clouds begin to gather?

A pencil, a pin, a soda straw, and a strip of paper make a weathervane.

Which way does the wind blow on a sunny day?

how fast does the wind blow?

How windy is it today? Weathermen find out by using an instrument called an anemometer to tell the speed of the wind.

You can make a model of an anemometer. Get four plastic foam cups, a long pencil, a sharp pin, crayons, and glue.

First, color one of the cups. Next, glue it and two others to the side of the fourth cup as shown in the photos. Make sure the three cups are evenly spaced about the center cup and that they face in the same direction. Place the center cup over the eraser of the pencil. Stick a pin through the cup into the eraser. Make sure the cup moves freely on the pin.

Take your anemometer outdoors and push the pencil staff into the ground. If you have a wrist watch with a second-hand, check to see how many times the colored cup turns around in one minute.

Compare the speed of the wind on different days. One day the colored cup may turn ten times in one minute. Another day the cup may make as many as sixty turns in one minute!

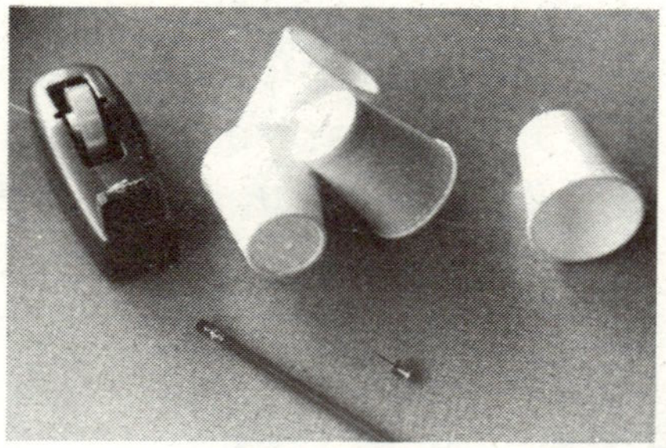

Peter Mongillo

To tell how fast the wind blows, make an anemometer.

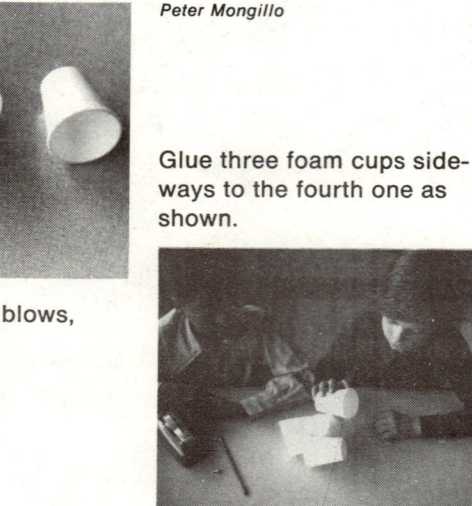

Glue three foam cups sideways to the fourth one as shown.

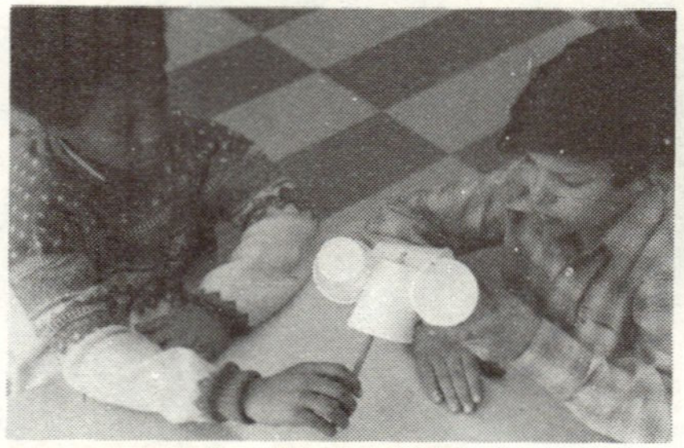

Set the anemometer outdoors, and count the number of times the colored cup turns in one minute.

Use the pin to fasten the center cup to the pencil.

fun at the beach

If you live near the seashore, you may make trips to the beach. And as a beachcomber, you can discover many kinds of marine plants and animals.

A great place to find some of these creatures is in a tide pool along a rocky shore. In a tide pool you may see sea snails, hermit crabs, periwinkles and sea anemones. These sea creatures wait for their food to be brought to them by the incoming tide.

Look carefully into the tide pool. How many kinds of creatures can you see? Do they move about or have they fastened themselves to the rocks. Are there shells or dead creatures in the pool?

Keep a record of the salt water creatures you see. If you pick one up, handle it gently, and then place it back in the tide pool. It belongs there!

A tide pool is a good place to look for sea creatures.

Try to find a whelk

One of the biggest shells on the beach is usually a spiral-shaped shell called a whelk. The shell may be found on many beaches along the Atlantic Coast. Sometimes you will find a living whelk inside the shell. The animal made the shell.

The adult whelk lays a string of egg cases like those shown in the photo. The eggs in each case hatch into young whelks. In time, the cases open and the tiny whelks come out. The whelk feeds on clams and other sea creatures. As the whelk grows, its shell grows larger. When the whelk becomes an adult, it will lay egg cases.

If you find an empty whelk shell, label it to tell where you found it. If the living whelk is still inside the shell, leave it on the beach.

Whelks lay strings of egg cases.

This spiral shell was made by a sea creature called a whelk.

A picture guide to shells

Would you like to find shells like those in the photo? If you are a good beachcomber, you may be able to. You can find shells hidden along beaches, riverbanks, and swamps. But the best places to look are the salt water beaches.

Shells look like different things. Some look like wings, cones, or paws. And others may be striped, spotted, or ribbed with many colors.

A soft-bodied creature made its home inside of every shell. The soft-bodied creature is called a mollusk. As the mollusk grows, the shell increases in size.

Most shells that you find belong to two main classes of the mollusk family. The two classes are called *univalves* and *bivalves*. The bivalves have two shells hinged together. Clams, mussels, oysters, and scallops belong to this class.

The shell of the univalve is spiral-shaped. As the mollusk grows, the spiral becomes larger. It may look like a cone or horn. Snails, conches, whelks and abalones belong to this class. You can find univalves in the forest or swamp, as well as at the beach.

Use this picture guide of shells to help you start a shell collection of your own. Set up your shell collection in a large cardboard box.

Florida State News Bureau

These are some of the many shells you may find on the beach.

Peek through a waterscope

Going swimming? Take along a waterscope to look into the secret world beneath the surface of the water.

To make a waterscope, start with an empty plastic bottle like the one in the photo. Cut off the bottom and the top of the bottle as shown. Now get a large sheet of plastic wrap.

Place the plastic over the bottom and sides of the bottle. Keep the plastic in place with a rubber band. Make sure the plastic wrap at the bottom of the bottle is smooth — no wrinkles. Now test the waterscope in a sink full of water. Look through the top of the bottle as if you were looking through a telescope. Check for leaks.

When at the beach, walk out a few feet into the water. Don't go out too far! Push the waterscope a few inches into the water. Look into the waterscope. What do you see?

You can make other waterscopes out of plastic pails, bottles, and even small wastebaskets. Which one makes the best waterscope?

You can make a waterscope from an empty plastic bottle. First, cut off the top of the bottle. Next, cut off the bottom. Put a sheet of plastic wrap over the bottom and up the sides of the bottle. Fasten it with a rubber band. Look through the top and check to see that the plastic on the bottom is smooth. Test your waterscope for leaks in a sink full of water.

Hunt for animal tracks

UPI photo

UPI photo

These tracks were made by some sea fowl walking on the beach. The tracks of sea birds on wet sand.

It can be exciting to study bird and animal footprints on a beach, along a stream, or after a snowfall. The tracks in the photos were made on a wet sandy beach. They were probably made by sea birds and ducks.

If you want to be a bird and animal tracker, start in your own neighborhood. Study footprints made by neighborhood dogs, cats, and other animals. Make a drawing to show what the tracks look like.

Of course, just after a snowfall is one of the best times to study tracks. You may be able to follow the tracks to find out where the animal went.

Take photographs of the tracks you find. Study animal tracks in nature books. See if you can learn what kind of animal makes what kind of tracks.

45

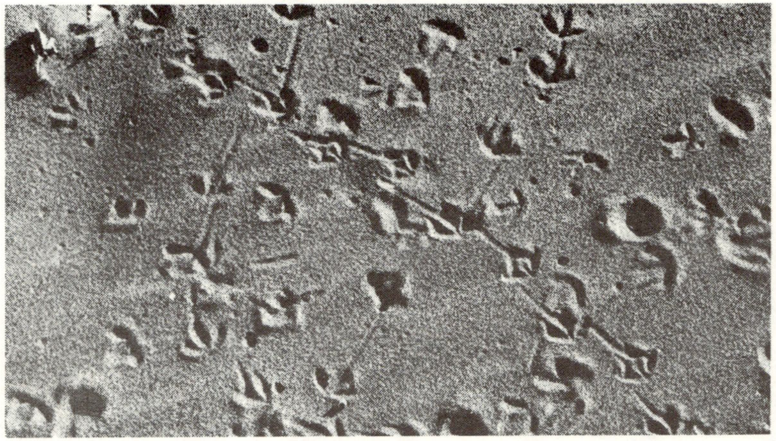

i see icicles

During the winter, icicles may be seen hanging from drainpipes, roofs, fences, and sometimes from the limbs of trees. You can have fun looking at icicles and learning about them.

On a cold day, get your friends together and go looking for the longest icicles you can find. Where did you find the longest one? Use a tape measure or a six-foot rule to measure the icicle.

If you can break it off, bring the icicle home. Put the icicle in a pail, bring it indoors, and weigh it. How much water did you get when the icicle melted?

Can you give some ideas on how icicles form?

UPI photo

Some of these icicles measured nearly two feet.

UPI photo

Icicles form a fringe on this lake guard-rail fence.

Frosty Fun

Wintertime is frosty fun time. Look for frost on window panes in your home. Use a magnifying lens to look closely at the icy decorations. You may see crystals that look like snowflakes.

The crystals were made from water vapor in the air. What happens to the crystal shapes when the windowpanes warm up? Breathe on the panes. What happens to your breath?

Add a touch of some water paint to the windowpane. Watch what happens. If you can, draw pictures of the crystal shapes.

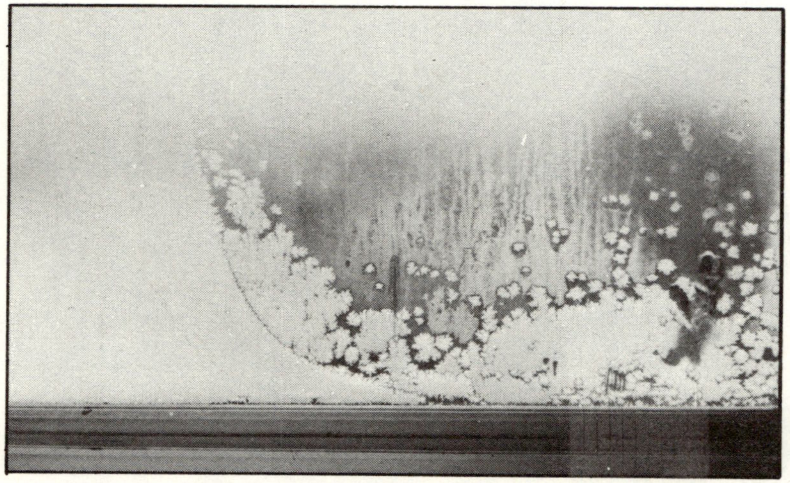

Use a magnifying lens to look closely at the window frost.

Look for frost on window panes in your house.